JAZZ PIANO SOLOS   VOLUME 27
late night jazz

Arranged by Brent Edstrom

T0071660

contents

ISBN 978-1-4584-2100-5

HAL•LEONARD®

Visit Hal Leonard Online at
www.halleonard.com

Contact us:
Hal Leonard
7777 West Bluemound Road
Milwaukee, WI 53213
Email: info@halleonard.com

In Europe, contact:
Hal Leonard Europe Limited
42 Wigmore Street
Marylebone, London, W1U 2RN
Email: info@halleonardeurope.com

In Australia, contact:
Hal Leonard Australia Pty. Ltd.
4 Lentara Court
Cheltenham, Victoria, 3192 Australia
Email: info@halleonard.com.au

ALMOST LIKE BEING IN LOVE

from BRIGADOON

Lyrics by ALAN JAY LERNER
Music by FREDERICK LOEWE

Slowly, with rubato

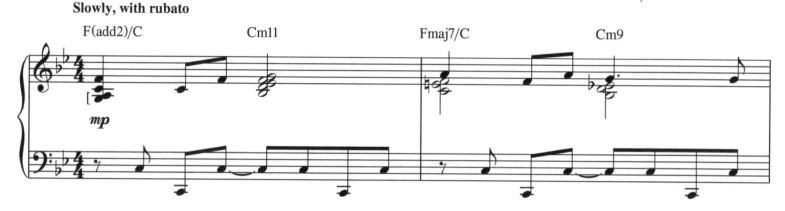

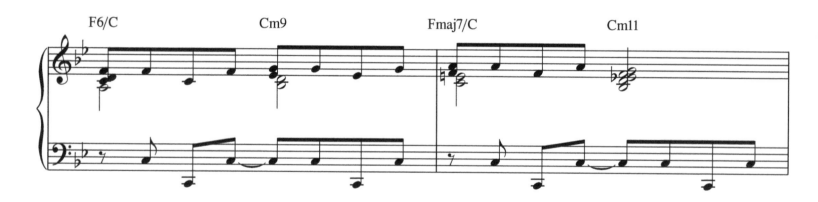

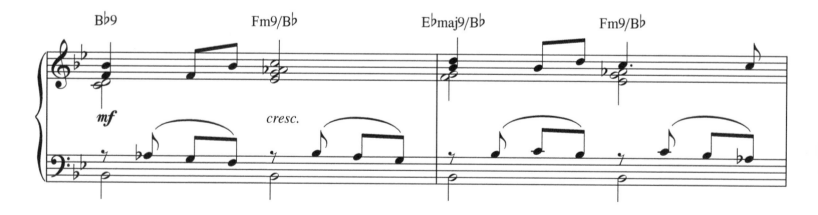

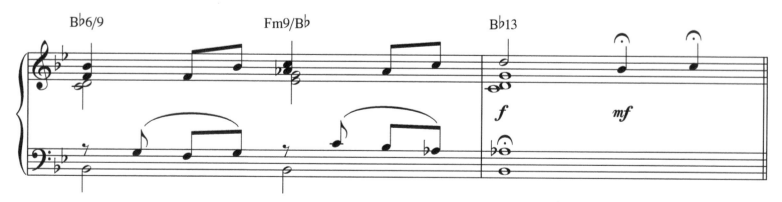

ANGEL EYES

Words by EARL BRENT
Music by MATT DENNIS

BEWITCHED
from PAL JOEY

Words by LORENZ HART
Music by RICHARD RODGERS

BLUE SKIES
from BETSY

Words and Music by
IRVING BERLIN

Fast Swing

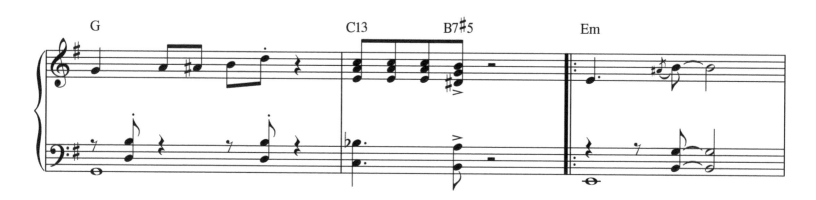

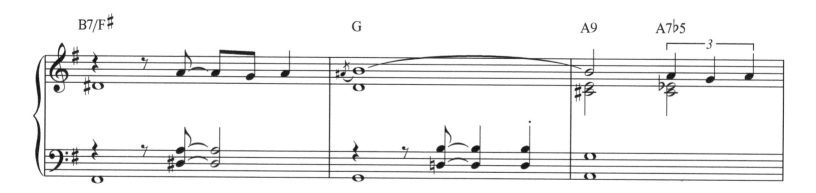

EVERYTHING HAPPENS TO ME

Words by TOM ADAIR
Music by MATT DENNIS

BYE BYE BLACKBIRD

from PETE KELLY'S BLUES

Lyric by MORT DIXON
Music by RAY HENDERSON

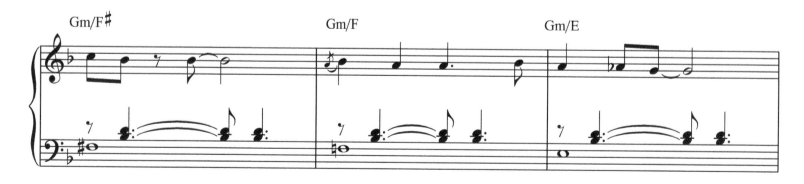

I WISH YOU LOVE

English Words by ALBERT BEACH
French Words and Music by CHARLES TRENET

Bossa

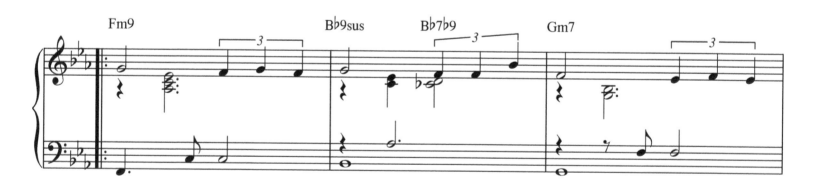

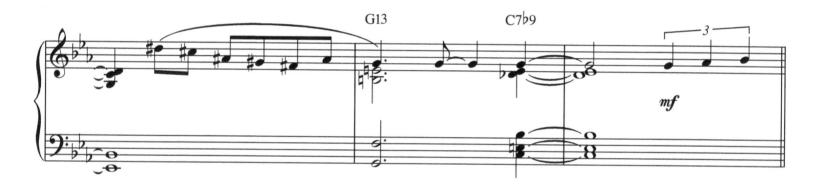

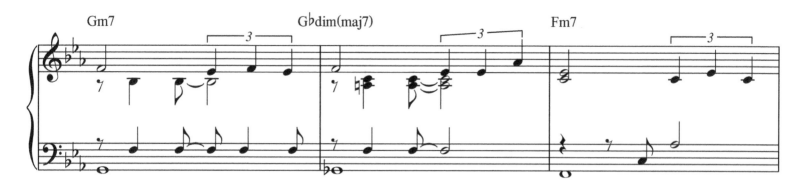

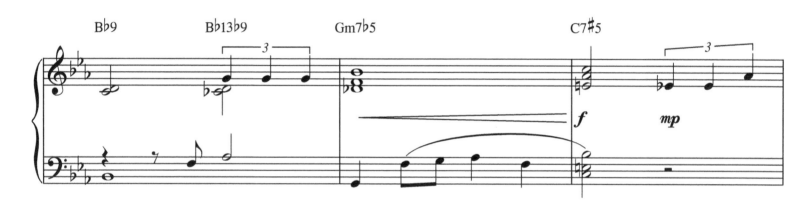

GOD BLESS' THE CHILD

Words and Music by ARTHUR HERZOG JR.
and BILLIE HOLIDAY

I WON'T DANCE

from ROBERTA

Words and Music by JIMMY McHUGH,
DOROTHY FIELDS, JEROME KERN,
OSCAR HAMMERSTEIN II and OTTO HARBACH

Bright Swing

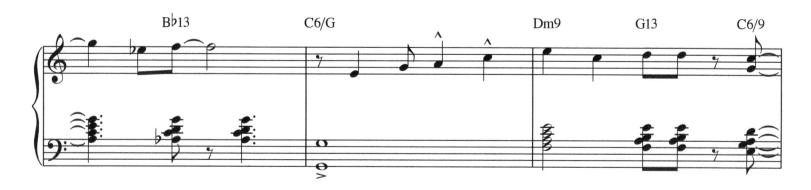

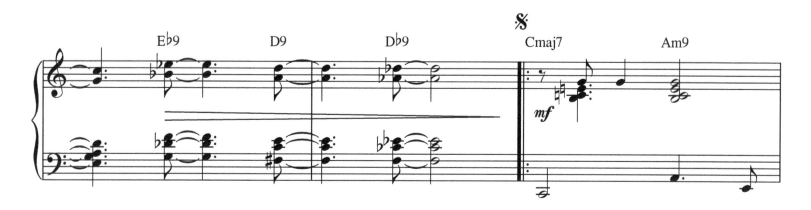

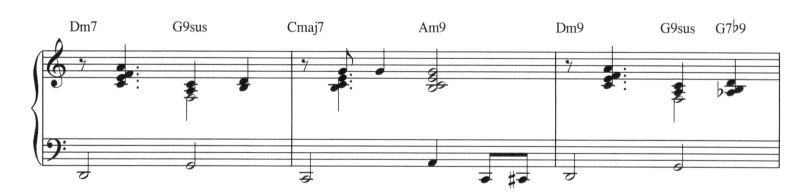

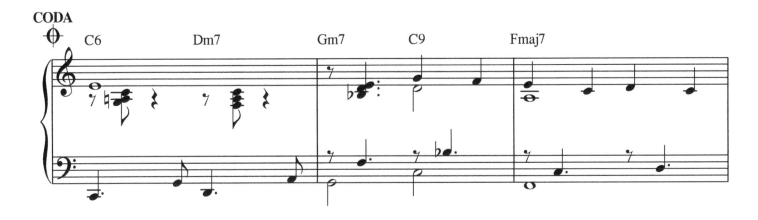

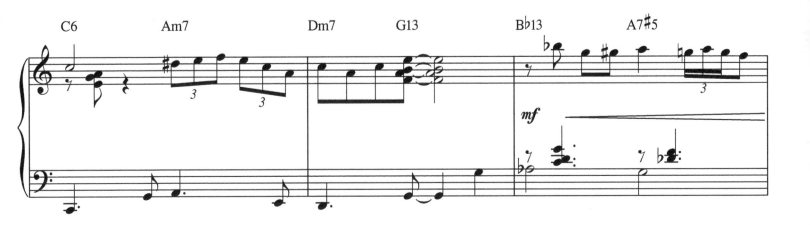

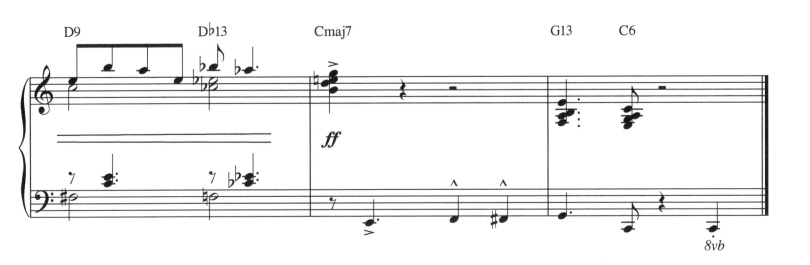

IF YOU COULD SEE ME NOW

Lyric by CARL SIGMAN
Music by TADD DAMERON

IF YOU GO AWAY

French Words and Music by JACQUES BREL
English Words by ROD McKUEN

Slowly

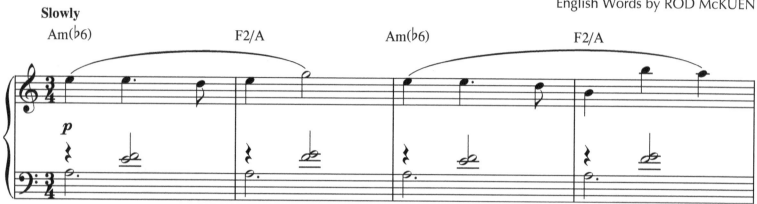

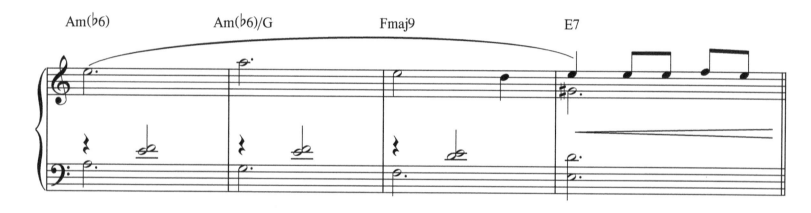

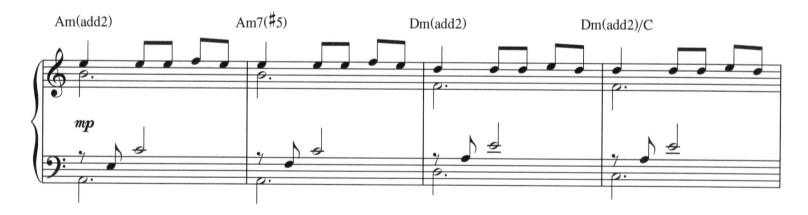

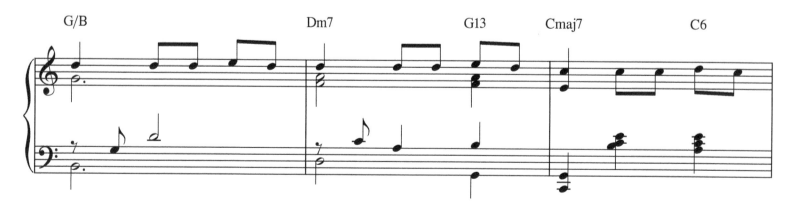

47

ILL WIND
(You're Blowin' Me No Good)
from COTTON CLUB PARADE

Lyric by TED KOEHLER
Music by HAROLD ARLEN

SMOKE GETS IN YOUR EYES

from ROBERTA

Words by OTTO HARBACH
Music by JEROME KERN

53

ISFAHAN
from FAR EAST SUITE

By DUKE ELLINGTON
and BILLY STRAYHORN

IT MIGHT AS WELL BE SPRING
from STATE FAIR

Lyrics by OSCAR HAMMERSTEIN II
Music by RICHARD RODGERS

LOVE ME OR LEAVE ME

Lyrics by GUS KAHN
Music by WALTER DONALDSON

ON GREEN DOLPHIN STREET

Lyrics by NED WASHINGTON
Music by BRONISLAU KAPER

THAT OLD BLACK MAGIC

from the Paramount Picture STAR SPANGLED RHYTHM

Words by JOHNNY MERCER
Music by HAROLD ARLEN

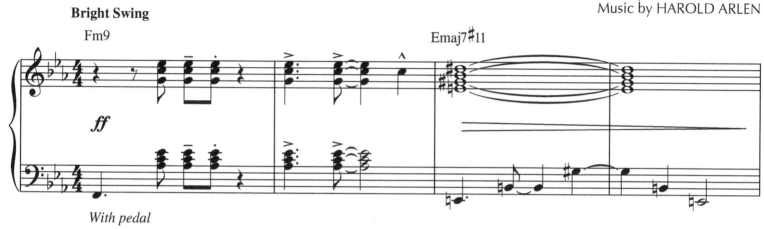

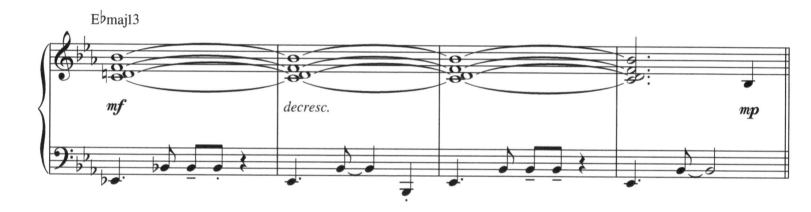

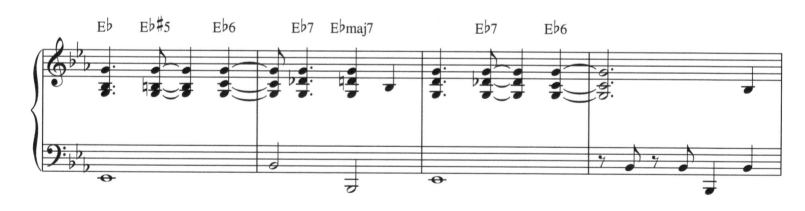

WHAT NOW MY LOVE

(Original French Title: "Et Maintenant")
Original French Lyric by Pierre Delano
Music by François Becaud
English Adaptation by Carl Sigman

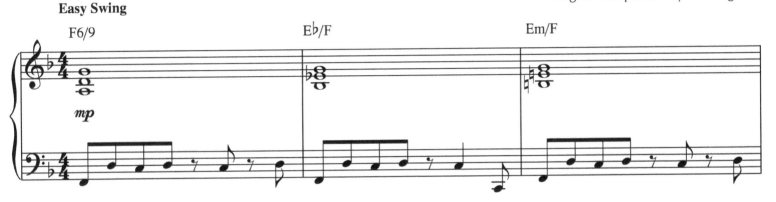

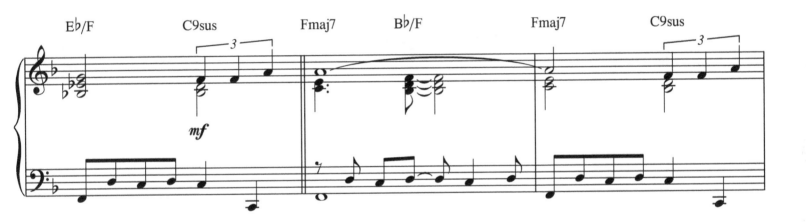

WHY WAS I BORN?

from SWEET ADELINE

Lyrics by OSCAR HAMMERSTEIN II
Music by JEROME KERN

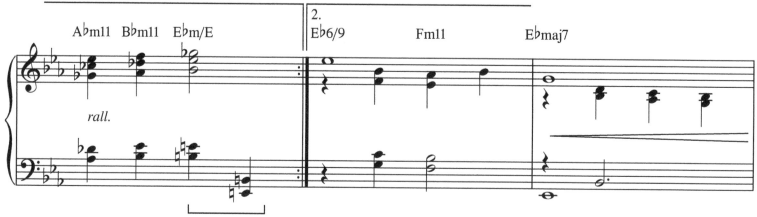

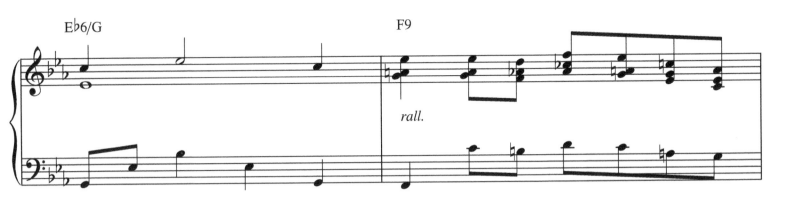

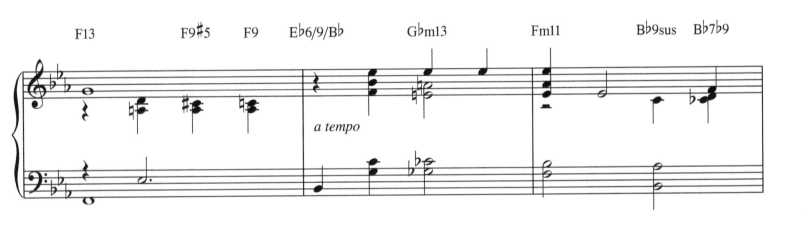

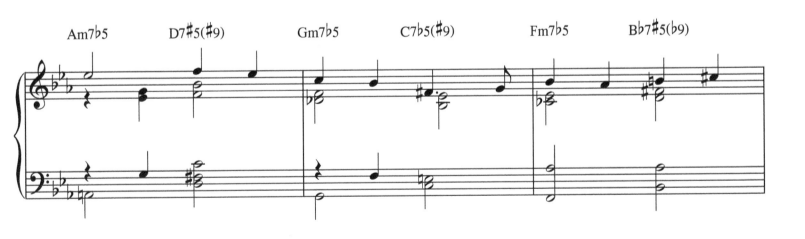

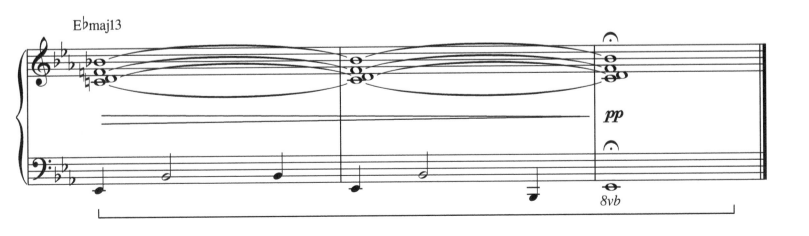

WILLOW WEEP FOR ME

Words and Music by
ANN RONELL

To Coda

WRAP YOUR TROUBLES IN DREAMS
(And Dream Your Troubles Away)

Lyric by TED KOEHLER and BILLY MOLL
Music by HARRY BARRIS

Bright Swing

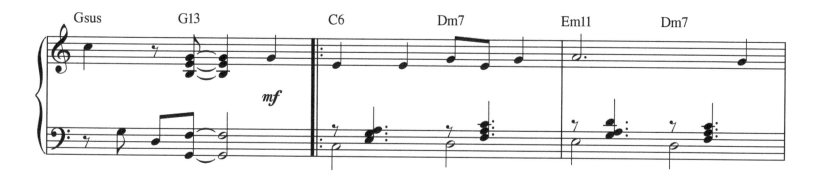

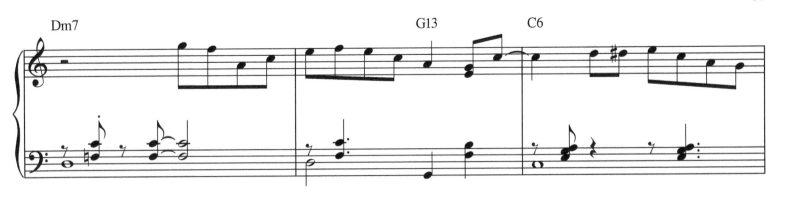

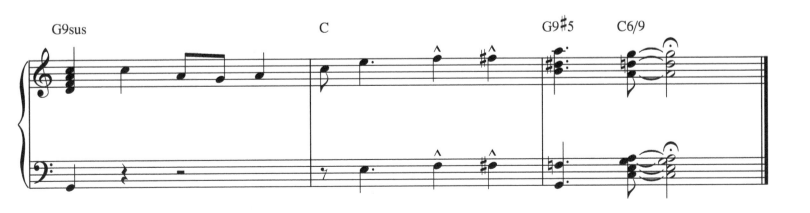

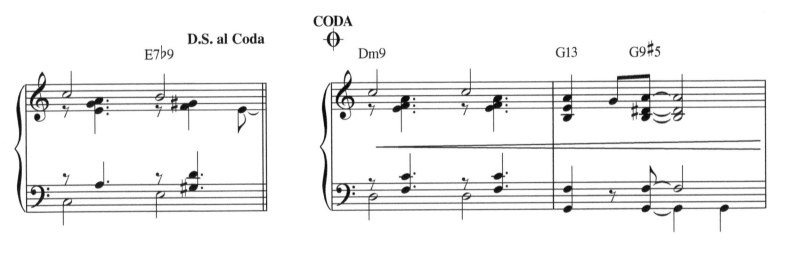

WHAT'S NEW?

Words by JOHNNY BURKE
Music by BOB HAGGART